IRISH LIFE AND CULTURE

II

POETRY
IN MODERN IRELAND

filíoċt éireannaċ na linne seo

le

aibistín ó cléiriġ

Arna maisiú ag

Luġaiḋ Le Brocquy, A.R.H.A.

POETRY
IN MODERN IRELAND

by

AUSTIN CLARKE

With illustrations by

LOUIS LE BROCQUY, A.R.H.A.

THE MERCIER PRESS, CORK

Poetry in Modern Ireland *is the second booklet in the series published for the Cultural Relations Committee of Ireland and was issued in 1951. For this second edition, the text has been revised and slightly lengthened in order to bring the essay up to date. The aim of the series is to give a broad, vivid and informed survey of Irish life and culture, past and present. Each writer is left free to deal with his subject in his own way, and the views expressed in any booklet are not necessarily those of the Committee.*

Austin Clarke is a distinguished poet in the generation that succeeded Yeats. His first book, The Vengeance of Fionn *was published in 1918, and his* Collected Poems *in 1936. He has also published other books of verse, poetic plays and three novels set in medieval Ireland. He has won a high reputation as an acute literary critic, for his original experiments in poetry, and as a pioneer of verse speaking in the Irish theatre and on Radio Eireann.*

ISBN 978 1 78117 936 9

Transferred to Digital Print-on-Demand in 2024

POETRY IN MODERN IRELAND

BY

AUSTIN CLARKE

I

IRISH POETRY ATTRACTED considerable attention in America, England and elsewhere during the early days of our literary movement, and, when we look back now, those far-off days seem almost legendary because of their eagerness and inspiration. The Irish Parliamentary Party was still at Westminster hoping to gain Home Rule by word of mouth. Everywhere the expectations of a new century had quickened new aims, but the immediate welcome given to our writers would not have been possible if they had not brought an imaginative quality of their own into poetry written in English. The enthusiasm with which Yeats, A.E., Synge and others were greeted in those legendary days could not have remained at its first high favour for the element of surprise and novelty cannot last.

5

When I went to London in the early 'twenties to earn my livelihood, I received a considerable shock. The elder writers, such as John Masefield, Walter de la Mare, Gordon Bottomley, G. K. Chesterton, had been enthusiastic about the Irish literary movement. But among the new Georgian poets and critics there was an impatience which almost amounted to a quiet boycott of Irish verse. The feeling was not entirely political. These writers, anxious to make names for themselves, resented the fashionable attention that had been given to us. They had adopted, in fact, a Sinn Fein policy of their own, and I could not but sympathise secretly with their attitude, because I realised for the first time that the ideal of literary independence was not purely a matter of national sentiment but of common-sense. In a household there are few guest-rooms, and even an affable guest cannot stay too long unless he marries into the family. Apart from that, the tradition of English poetry is as exclusive as that of the old Bardic system in Ireland. Moore, Mangan, Ferguson, de Vere, Allingham, at their best, have never been really included in its canon. Recently, when English modernists and traditionalists were engaged in alarming scuffles among themselves, our quiet neutral speech had little chance of a hearing: even Yeats, in his later years, was not recognised as an Irish poet, but as an important convert to either or both contending schools.

Owing to present confusion and neglect, the particular conditions of our poetry are often misunderstood—indeed the fact that critics speak of an Irish literary revival shows in itself a certain measure of inaccuracy. We do not speak of an English, French or American literary revival and, in the strict sense of the word, therefore, it is inaccurate to speak of an Irish literary revival. The movement which expanded so quickly, so imaginatively, at the beginning of the present century was the result of a gradual development. We can trace that development back to the eighteenth century when the English language spread more widely throughout Ireland and the native language and its literature were in decline. That double influence, direct or indirect, sometimes obscure, sometimes clear, is still with us. But the new movement had all the excitement of a revival, and the first phase of modern Irish literature is remarkable for the fact that so many of our writers, both in prose and verse, were preoccupied with mythology. Standish James O'Grady, Yeats, A.E., William Larminie, James Stephens, Katherine Tynan and others, all explored, in different ways, our heroic age. Few of them knew the Irish language, but, in re-discovering for themselves, excitedly, the mythology, sagas, and oral tradition of their own country, they had for stimulus the pioneer work of scholars and neglected poet-translators. In turning to our ancient sources, they broke from the main tradition of English poetry, which has for centuries borrowed its mythology from Greece and Rome.

Imaginative interest in mythology, saga and folklore is due, of course, to the romantic movement which spread throughout Europe at the beginning of the nineteenth century. That interest had been latent in Anglo-Irish literature, but it was stirred again into fresh expression by the Gaelic material which our writers were discovering directly or indirectly for themselves. In order to deal, however, with all this mass of tradition, they had to turn away deliberately from the modern age of realism, Seen, therefore, from a broader point of view, the movement here might be described as one of the last delayed trends of European romanticism. Lord Dunsany

7

invented a mythology for himself, and James Joyce, feeling at last the same need of mythology, turned to one of the epics of Homer. It would be too much to claim that our elder poets anticipated the present mythological movement in European literature, but in England, France, and elsewhere there has been an increasing interest in mythology, partly due to the psychological exploration of sub-conscious symbolism by Freud and others—an interest confined mainly to the classical era. The poetic mythology of France, like that of England, has always been borrowed from classical literature, and contemporary French poets and playwrights have returned to the themes of Greek tragedy to find symbol and similitude for the present woeful state of the human race. A mere list of names indicates how powerful has been this urge, for the list includes Jean Cocteau, Giradoux, Anouilh, Sartre, Camus.

In returning to Irish mythology, our poets experienced an emotion which was unknown to English poets, an emotion which gives their work its peculiar intensity. They were not exploring a borrowed mythology, but one which belonged to their country, survived in its oral tradition, and in the very names of its hills, rivers and plains. When Keats turned to Greek mythology, he went to Lemprière's Classical Dictionary; our poets went out of doors. We can estimate the intensity of this emotional experience by the fact that our elder writers never escaped from its influence. One of the early poems of A.E., for example, deals with Dana, the *Mater Deorum* in Irish mythology. At that time Yeats and he were influenced by American transcendentalism and in particular by Emerson's doctrine of the Oversoul. So, A.E. based his lyric on Emerson's well-known poem, *Brahma,*

8

"I am the slayer and the slain," mingling in its general theme particular reference to that note of heroic generosity which is found in our sagas.

> I breathe
> A deeper pity than all love, myself
> Mother of all, but without hands to heal,
> Too vast and vague—they know me not! But yet
> I am the heartbreak over fallen things,
> The sudden gentleness that stays the blow;
> And I am in the kiss that warriors give
> Pausing in battle, and in the tears that fall
> Over the vanquished foe; and in the highest
> Among the Danaan gods I am the last
> Council of mercy in their hearts, where they
> Mete justice from a thousand starry thrones.

In 1934, A.E. published his last book of poems but, despite its title, *The House of the Titans*, it has no reference to classical mythology. The title poem is, in fact, a long narrative, dealing with the ancient Irish gods, and its Asiatic thought reminds us that our mythology originally came from the East. The fact that the early lyrical passage from which I have quoted is embodied in this last narrative is surely not without significance. The case of Yeats is even more remarkable, for his later poetry shows an ever-increasing diversity of interests and themes: yet despite all this diversity, the poet kept returning to mythology and saga. One of his first poems was entitled *The Death of Cuchulain*; later he dealt with the same theme in his play, *On Baile's Strand*; and in his last play, also called *The Death of Cuchulain*, we find him writing once more on the epic theme of the Ulster hero. So, at the age of seventy-three, he went back to the tale which he had used almost fifty years before. His second last play, *The Herne's Egg*, also deals with a mythological subject and explores fantastically the Celtic doctrine of transmigration. There is a curious fact about these two last plays which has not been observed: the story of *The Herne's Egg* and the episode of the Fool in *The Death of Cuchulain* are both to be found in *Congal*, the epic poem, which Samuel Ferguson published in 1872. I mention this because some recent English critics have suggested that the Irish literary movement, in its early phase, was little more than a leakage from the pre-Raphaelite School. Undoubtedly the youthful Yeats learned much of his art from the pre-Raphaelite School and was encouraged by the immediate fact that his friend, William Morris, was turning to the Teutonic sagas. But his declared object was to reform Irish verse which had become declamatory and almost entirely political in its interest. He followed the way of Ferguson, the first of our poets to write in the epic manner, but he lacked the advantage of the elder poet, who was a Gaelic scholar and could range at will for his themes. The only long narrative poem which Yeats wrote, *The Wanderings of Usheen*, was due to a happy chance. It was directly inspired by an eighteenth-century Gaelic poem of Micheál Coimín, *Laoidh Oisín i dTír na n-Óg*, and ten years before Yeats's book appeared, a translation of that lay had been published by the Ossianic Society. This shows how considerably our poets have profited from the labours of our scholars. Yeats came from London to write his poem in Sligo: there he could look across the Atlantic waters, over which his hero had journeyed with Niamh, and a few miles to the north he could see Ben Gulbain, a mountain still associated in local tradition with the legends of Oisin. We can find in the poem, of course, the refining influence of pre-Raphaelite poetry, but there is a difference. I remember visiting Sligo in the winter-time and noting how accurately the poet had described western sky and ocean-tide. 'The dove-grey edge of the sea,' for example, no longer seemed a purely literary phrase: it was an exact description of the extraordinarily delicate colours I saw, and the adjective 'pearl-pale,' which the poet was to use so often, exactly defined the moist, iridescent airs.

English nature poetry is so contemplative and personal that we can sympathise at times with Wordsworth's surprising exclamation:

> Great God ! I'd rather be
> A pagan suckled in a creed outworn—
> So might I, standing on this pleasant lea,
> Have glimpses that would make me less forlorn;
> Have sight of Proteus rising from the sea;
> Or hear old Triton blow his wreathed horn.

But in those early and enthusiastic days Irish poets seemed to enjoy a continuous vision of a land populated exclusively with mythological beings. In 1901, Herbert Trench published his narrative poem, *Deirdre Wed,* a work which has something of the epic strength of Ferguson at his best. In this poem the story is set in Connemara, where Deirdre and her lover take refuge at first among the glens over-shadowed by Muilrea and Bengorm. At times the wild loveliness of the heroine might almost be that of the landscape itself, that dark region linked by many waters:

> Tall as a rush is she,
> Sweet as the glitter of the netted lakes.

This mingling of landscape and lore, this topographical excitement, as we might call it, was the expression of a new emotional experience, but the experience itself was not enough to differentiate our poetry from English tradition. All these writers had a literary ideal of their own, for, in varying degrees, they were trying to capture something of the imaginative quality which is to be found in early Gaelic poetry and saga. In the 'sixties, the Victorian poet and critic, Matthew Arnold, published his well-known and much-discussed essay, *On the Study of Celtic Literature.* He discerned in Gaelic and Welsh nature poetry a remarkable grace, delicacy and verbal magic, and wherever he found such qualities in English literature from Shakespeare onwards, he attributed them to a pervasive Celtic strain. His theory may have been extravagant, but long afterwards it enabled a younger generation of Irish poets to recognise such qualities in their own early literature and make of them a literary ideal. When Standish Hayes O'Grady published his *Silva Gadelica* in 1892, he gave to poets of the future an immense treasury of imaginative material. When I was at school I groped with dim excitement through an Irish mediaeval tale entitled *Eisirt,* a tale from which Swift is supposed to have borrowed his idea of Lilliput. Later I learned to appreciate its fascinating mixture of lore and imagery. Here are a few lines from a poem in it, translated by O'Grady :

> Burn not the precious apple-tree of spreading and low-sweeping bough; tree ever decked in bloom of white, against whose fair head all men put forth the hand. The surly blackthorn is a wanderer, and a wood that the artificer burns not : throughout its body, though it be scanty, birds in their flocks warble. The noble willow

12

burn not, a tree sacred to poems : with his bloom bees are a sucking, all love the little cage. The graceful tree with the berries, the wizards' tree, the rowan, burn : but spare the limber tree : burn not the slender hazel.

The late Robin Flower, the English poet and scholar, who was Keeper of the Gaelic Manuscripts in the British Museum, never completed his projected work on Gaelic literature, but part of it, entitled *The Irish Tradition*, was edited and published posthumously in 1947. In this study Dr. Flower shows that the men who made the sagas for us had an exquisite sensitiveness to external impressions :

> They possessed that Celtic art of isolating and defining those impressions in brief and decisive sentences which in the last analysis gives their abiding charm to the best of the Welsh and Irish writings.

He takes in illustration an episode from the *Táin Bó Fraích*, a tale perhaps of the eight century. Queen Maeve and her husband Ailill have instructed Fraoch, son of a fairy woman and the lover of their daughter, Findabhair, to swim in a monster-haunted pool. He is about to leave the water unharmed when Ailill bids him back :

> ' Come not out of the water,' said Ailill, ' until thou bring me a branch from yonder rowan tree on the river's brink. For its berries are beautiful to me.' Fraoch returns and breaks a branch from the tree and brings it on his back across the water. And Findabhair cried out : ' Is that not beautiful to see ? ' For beautiful it was to her to see Fraoch over the dark water, the body so white, the hair so lovely, the face so shapely, the eye of deep

13

grey, and all the tender youth faultless and without blame, his face narrow below and broad above, his straight and flawless make, the branch with the crimson berries between the throat and the white face.

In the words of Dr. Flower: "that vision so clearly seen, so surely and swiftly rendered is of the very heart of the saga literature." It is from such glimpses and gleams of a lost art that our poets were gradually to learn. We owe much to the discernment of Matthew Arnold, but his stimulating study was actually inspired by Renan's famous Essay on the Poetry of the Celtic Races. Renan was a Breton and could write, therefore, not only with direct knowledge but with imaginative feeling. So we may attribute, perhaps, the original impulse which set our poets busy to the great scholar, stylist, and sceptic, whose biblical criticism caused such a sensation in nineteenth-century France.

II

The unexpected is almost always the rule in literary movements, so involved is the interplay of influences both from the past and present, so powerful the self-development that genius demands. Yeats and his fellow poets were essentially lyrical and so their discovery of the Irish mythological and heroic age did not result, as we might expect, in epic poems. They were attracted by the vestiges of that mythology which still lingered in remote places, for the fairies of local superstition are but dwindled memories of the powerful beings who move throughout the ancient stories. Romantic interest in such obscure country belief was responsible for that unexpected phase, that diversion of the literary movement known to us as the Celtic Twilight. In English poetry the fairy faith found in the old ballads had long since vanished—even in the time of Shakespeare, Drayton and Herrick the sprites were only diminutive creatures of fancy. But in brooding over our surviving fairy lore, these new Irish poets brought back imaginative feeling to a theme that had come to be regarded as merely playful. They had discovered, for good or bad, the people of the Sidhe.

The mood of mystery had been anticipated by Samuel Ferguson in his lyrical Ulster ballad, *The Fairy Thorn*, in which he tells how three girls, who dance at dusk around the forbidden tree, are drawn within the ring of enchantment. I remember A.E. quoting to me the stanzas in this poem which had inspired Yeats and himself because of their twilight hue and a vowel-music suggested by Gaelic internal assonance.

> They're glancing through the glimmer of the quiet eve,
> Away in milky wavings of neck and ankle bare;
> The heavy-sliding stream in its sleepy song they leave,
> And the crags in the ghostly air.

The dance ends in a dread hush:

> Thus clasped and prostrate all, with their heads together
>   bowed,
> Soft o'er their bosoms beating—the only human sound—
> They hear the silky footsteps of the silent fairy crowd,
> Like a river in the air gliding round.

In that way began the fairy music which Yeats and others were to develop so persistently and express in such delicate wayward rhythms.

When I first discovered for myself the Celtic Twilight, as a young student, and read the poems of that period, much was quite incomprehensible to me. I groped through a mist of blurred meanings, stumbled over lines in which every accent seemed to be in the wrong place. It was all quite unlike English poetry and quite unlike that Gaelic poetry which Dr. Douglas Hyde declaimed for us in class, excitedly jumping from the rostrum step to the floor and back again. When I had made, however, the Grand Tour of English literature, the difficulties were gone. It was pleasant to escape awhile from the mighty law and order of English poetry into that shadowy world of subdued speech and nuance. But the rapid spread of that Celtic Twilight mood was due accidentally to the visionary power of George Russell, better known to us as A.E. Drawn towards eastern religious thought and gnosticism, he devoted himself to mystical contemplation and almost hesitated to write poetry lest it prove to be an earthly pursuit. His first book of poems, published modestly under the pseudonym of A.E., had an extraordinary maturity, for in it form and expression were completely unified. This was a rare achievement, when we realise that the poet was only twenty-seven years of age. The very title of the book, *Homeward Thoughts by the Way*, is significant, for the poet, believing that the human soul, in this mortal life, is finding its way back to a former greatness, expressed in it the longing for eternity. The insubstantiality of this world is suggested by the very imagery, jewel-like, yet dissolving, drawn from the many-coloured sky-changes of evening.

16

Its edges foamed with amethyst and rose,
Withers once more the old blue flower of day:
There where the ether like a diamond glows
    Its petals fade away.

A shadowy tumult stirs the dusky air;
Sparkle the delicate dews, the distant snows;
The great deep thrills, for through it everywhere
    The breath of Beauty blows.

In *Dana* we find the same dusking:

            I weave
My spells at evening, folding with dim caress,
Aerial arms, and twilight-dropping hair,
The lonely wanderer by shore or wood,
Till filled with some vast tenderness he yields,
Feeling in dreams for the dear mother heart
He knew ere he forsook the starry way.

In this renunciation of the earth there was an implied quietism.

What of all the will to do?
It has vanished long ago,
For a dream-shaft pierced it through
From the Unknown Archer's bow.

The mood lasted into the new century and we can trace it even in such a poem as *In the Seven Woods* by Yeats, for all the sunlit imagery.

I am contented, for I know that Quiet
Wanders laughing and eating her wild heart
Among pigeons and bees, while that Great Archer,
Who but waits His hour to shoot, still hangs
A cloudy quiver over Parc-na-lee.

With A.E. that other-worldly mood was one of spiritual belief:

> I am the tender voice calling ' Away,'
> Whispering between the beatings of the heart.

But it is Yeats who brings us back to the objects of the Irish literary movement and to the new interest in fairy lore.

> The host is riding from Knocknarea
> And over the grave of Clooth-na-Bare;
> Caoilte tossing his burning hair
> And Niamh calling Away, come away.

Lacking faith, but feeling that he needed more than imaginative justification for his interest in fairies, ghosts, spirits, Yeats sought confirmation in magical circles, table-rapping and psychic research. All that doubtful enquiry gave peculiar intensity to his early poems and yet they lack the stir of deep conflict. His poetic play, *The Land of Heart's Desire*, tells of the fairy abduction of a young bride and, despite its deliberate naiveté, is strangely moving. But four years after that play was published in the 'nineties, a terrible event happened in a remote corner of Co. Tipperary, which brings back to us the grim realities of superstition. A young woman was burned alive by her husband and relatives in the belief that her own body and mind were absent and that they were expelling a fairy changeling. The trial was held at the Clonmel Assizes in 1895. Here, in its pity, terror, and cruel bewilderment of ignorance, was the real poetic tragedy.

As a literary phase, a passing experience, the twilight mood was fast becoming a vogue, so that soon all that is vague, wistful and dreamful was assumed to be characteristic of the Celtic race here and elsewhere. The attraction of the mood was due to the fact that it expressed, in remote imagery, a distinct tendency towards world-weariness at the close of the last century. Ernest Dowson, Arthur Symons, and other English writers, who were friends of Yeats, were aware sensitively of the *fin de siècle* movement on the Continent and the influence of Maeterlinck was spreading. In France, Verlaine, Samain, de Regnier, had turned from strident realism to a poetry of nuance, suggestion and faint symbolism; and in painting, also, there were fugitive hues—the immateriality of impressionism. So, in abandoning for a while the fundamental commonsense of English poetic tradition, our poets set themselves free for curious mental experience, and rendered themselves liable to many intermingling influences. In the love-poetry of Yeats the Twilight mood resulted in a rare delicacy of exalted thought and simple word.

> You need but lift a pearl-pale hand,
> And bind up your long hair and sigh;
> And all men's hearts must burn and beat;
> And candle-like foam on the dim sand,
> And stars climbing the dew-dropping sky,
> Live but to light your passing feet.

With imaginative discrimination, the poet developed those slow-delaying rhythms which Callanan, Ferguson and others gave us in their translations from Gaelic poetry. Curiously enough, Thomas Moore had found those rhythms accidentally, when setting words to Irish folk music, in such poems as *Through Grief and through Danger thy smile hath cheer'd my way*, and *At the mid hour of night, when stars were weeping, I fly*. These evasive rhythms were a novelty in the English language, though they had been known to Thomas Campion, the Elizabethan lyric poet and composer.

Soon the fashion of the Celtic Twilight spread so much that it seemed as if all our poetry must hurry us, mortals, into a dim, invisible world—all words must be an attempt to capture the music of the Sidhe, as in this gay-sad lilt by Nora Hopper:

All the way to Tir na n'Og are many roads that run,
But the darkest road is trodden by the King of Ireland's
    Son.
The world wears on to sundown, and love is lost and won,
But he recks not of loss or gain, the King of Ireland's
    Son,
He follows on for ever, when all your chase is done,
He follows after shadows—the King of Ireland's Son.

Elsewhere the mood was attracting many and we can find its influence in Scotland not only in the prose and verse of William Sharp, who wrote under the pseudonym of Fiona Macleod, but also, with ironic implications, in some of the work of J. M. Barrie. In England it stirred Lionel Johnson, who was of Irish descent, Arthur Symons, Arthur Machen, and others. G. K. Chesterton paid tribute to it in his play, *Magic*, and, as we may suspect, it stimulated Walter de la Mare to evoke an English Twilight of his own. To some the success of the Celtic Twilight may recall the eighteenth century craze for Macpherson's *Ossian*, those dim, misty prose poems, which purported to be translations from Gaelic manuscripts, and were part of the first stirrings of European romanticism. Nevertheless, we cannot but admire the remarkable courage of Yeats who led the assault upon commonsense, striving tenaciously to confirm his faith in fairies, despite plain opposition, by every self-deceiving device of naiveté and sophistry.

All literary phases tend towards extremes and the inevitable reaction against the Celtic Twilight has obscured from us some of its interesting qualities. The attempt to suggest other-worldly moods by verbal music and imagery led to the perfecting of a conscious art at a time when the aesthetic doctrine of Pater and Wilde was still prevalent. But for the moment the original aims of the literary movement were almost forgotten. Nothing could be further than this new poetry from the patriotic, historical ballads of the Young Ireland school, written in the haste of revolutionary action during the 1840's, by Thomas Davis, Charles Gavan Duffy, Thomas D'Arcy Magee and others. Nothing could be further from the vigorous rhetorical manner of that propaganda verse, which, with all its faults, had survived in popular tradition through copious imitation. Nothing could be less representative of a country which was trying to forget as quickly as it could the old semi-pagan beliefs still lingering in remote districts. Alike in its interests, its function, and technique, the new poetry had broken away from general opinion. Nevertheless there are aspects of the Celtic Twilight which should not be ignored, for its expresses at times for us the melancholy solitude of depopulated places, hinting at the long centuries of opposition, exile and despair, as in these lines by Seamus O'Sullivan:

> It is a whisper among the hazel bushes;
> It is a long low whispering voice that fills
> With a sad music the bending and swaying rushes;
> It is a heart beat deep in the quiet hills.

Twilight people, why will you still be crying,
Crying and calling to me out of the trees?
For under the quiet grass the wise are lying,
And all the strong ones are gone over the seas.

Moreover, there is another quality in the poetry of the Celtic
Twilight School which has been overlooked, a quality that
may be described as imaginative realism. English poetry
has borrowed its skies so often from Greece and Rome that
much of it exists in an ideal sunshine and we have to return
almost to the Anglo-Saxon alliterative staves to find the lost
mists and twilight of the northern latitude. Verlaine, Verhaeren
and other foreign poets who visited England have described
its skies in the gloomiest lines, but in the Celtic Twilight
writers we find a continual awareness of all the cloudiness
and half-light of the north. Yeats, in his masterly way, could
express in a single line the very atmosphere of Connaught:

A wet wind blowing out of the clinging air—
And in a couple of lines evoke the loneliness of legend-
haunted hills—

The wind has bundled up the clouds high over Knocknarea
And thrown the thunder on the stones for all that Maeve
can say.

The legendary music of the Sidhe was not to be expelled
without difficulty, and even after the Rising of 1916, we find
Yeats still enthralled by it, though his poetry had become austere.

At the grey round of the hill
Music of a lost kingdom
Runs, runs and is suddenly still.
The winds out of Clare-Galway
Carry it: suddenly it is still.

22

I have heard in the night air
A wandering airy music;
And moidered in that snare
A man is lost of a sudden,
In that sweet wandering snare.

My own contemporary, F. R. Higgins, wrote a good-humoured farewell to the fairies in a ballad written in the traditional manner. He tells how he meets a fairy-woman near Gort, a few miles away from Lady Gregory's demesne, where Yeats wrote so much of his poetry. Cunningly she entices him with a promise of an unlimited supply of illicit liquor but he resists her blandishments.

> " Then live with me, man, and I will give you
>   The run of twelve hills with a still in each."
> Her eyes were craving that rainy evening
>   While a gentle air was in her speech.
>
> But O, my darling, who is your father?
>   Ah, would your mother take kindly to me?"
> And then she told me, " My folk ride over
>   The sliver flowering of a green-lit sea."
>
> At those strange words then I did remember
>   Her folk they were of no good sort,
> So I bid good evening to that young woman
>   And she took herself to the woods of Gort !

III

The rapid vogue of the Celtic Twilight at the turn of the century concealed for a while the real direction of our poetry. But other influences were astir and the increasing effort of enthusiasts to save the Irish language was to affect in many ways a new generation of writers. When Douglas Hyde published the oral poetry which he had collected in the Irish-speaking districts of Connacht, he revealed suddenly

to those young writers an entire imaginative tradition, for
these poems had developed obscurely through centuries from
Gaelic literature itself. His two collections, *The Love Songs
of Connacht,* and *The Religious Songs of Connacht,* were
bi-lingual publications, because in order to help those who
were learning the language, he included a translation both of
the poems and the commentary which he had written in
simplest western Irish. Fortunately, Douglas Hyde was a
poet and the best of the hasty translations that he made in
verse showed something of the imaginative quality of the
originals. Moreover, by a happy chance, he preserved the
idiom of the Gaelic sentences not only in his literal prose
versions of many of the poems, but also in the translation
of his commentary.

That happy chance was to have unforeseen consequences,
for the curious prose, both in its rhythm and idiom, was to
inspire Synge and give him the very means of elaborating his
own dialogue. Incidentally we may mention, too, that
one of Hyde's humorous little plays in Irish, translated by
Lady Gregory and known later as *The Workhouse Ward,*
was to be the start, for better or worse, of the popular peasant
comedies of the Abbey Theatre.

The poems themselves came to a younger generation with
a note that was strange and rare; and in some of his versions
Hyde indicated the internal pattern by rhyme:

A honey mist on a day of frost, in a dark oak wood,
And love for thee in my heart in me, thou bright,
    white, and good;
Thy slender form, soft and warm, thy red lips apart,
Thou hast found me, and hast bound me, and put
    grief in my heart.

Although unequal, the translations showed the directness of a lost mode:

> Ringleted youth of my love,
>   With thy locks bound loosely behind thee,
> You passed by the road above,
>   But you never came in to find me;
> Where were the harm for you
>   If you came for a little to see me,
> Your kiss is a wakening dew
>   Were I ever so ill or so dreamy.

Most of these anonymous poems had been composed in the century and a half between the Williamite wars and the Famine which swept away so much tradition. Here, in the *Love Songs,* were the young in those far-off times as they saw themselves, struggling against an emotion which freed and bound them at the same time. They saw before them, in their own words, " the star of knowledge," but they were oppressed by custom and their own bewilderment. They longed for early marriage and for their own choice, but they were frustrated by poverty and match-making. Fear of scandal, betrayal, sorrow and shame—these were their themes, and a traditional skill had given to their expression a simple, yet passionate directness:

> You have taken east and you have taken west from me,
> You have taken the path before me and the path behind me,
> You have taken moon and you have taken sun from me,
> And great is my fear that you have taken God from me!

These lines are from a poem taken down in Munster and I quote the English rendering by Padraic Pearse to show how this influence was to spread in the early years of the century.

Padraic Colum, Joseph Campbell and others were quick to learn from the emotion of these poems. With fine instinct they avoided the dangers of dialect—even Synge, when he wrote verse, abandoned the idiomatic phrases which he collected from island and glen for his plays. Following the example of Allingham and Yeats, who had learned from the traditional ballads in English, they relied on simple natural speech, blending into it occasional country phrases with subtle care. In such a poem as *The Poor Girl's Meditation* by Padraic Colum the original emotion has passed so quietly in English that we scarcely realise that it is a translation:

> And, O young lad that I love,
> I am no mark for your scorn;
> All you can say of me is
> Undowered I was born:
> And if I've no fortune in hand,
> Nor cattle and sheep of my own,
> This I can say, O lad,
> I am fitted to lie my lone !

Developing this recovered mode, Colum could suggest in *A Poor Scholar of the 'Forties* the very clash between politics and divergent traditions:

> And I must walk this road that winds
> 'Twixt bog and bog, while east there lies
> A city with its men and books;
> With treasures open to the wise,
> Heart-words from equals, comrade-looks;
> > Down here they have but tale and song,
> > They talk Repeal the whole night long.

In the north Joseph Campbell had disciplined himself by setting words to traditional Irish airs collected by Herbert Hughes, and that discipline is shown in the pure line of many an early lyric, such as, "I will go with my father a-ploughing." He was inspired mostly by the religious folk songs, but he learned something also from the Gaelic lore and ranns of Scotland. His lines are sparse and brief:

> I am the gilly of Christ
> The mate of Mary's Son;
> I run the roads at seeding time,
> And when the harvest's done.
>
> I sleep among the hills,
> The heather is my bed;
> I dip the termon-well for drink,
> And pull the sloe for bread . . .

Like Synge, these poets were aware of a rapidly passing tradition and had trained themselves in order to express something of its fullness. Their deliberate aim is made quite clear by Joseph Campbell who refers in prefatory verses both to *The Vision of Piers Plowman* and to the lyrics of Herrick. We are reminded that in the fourteenth century, in a last revolt against a changing age, Langland had evoked a mediaeval folk life, and that long after, Herrick was inspired by the old customs and lore which were to disappear so rapidly with the triumph of Puritanism. But the revival of the Irish language, the growth of nationalism, and their own joy in writing, gave these poets both hope and confidence. Taking the word 'Irishry,' which had been bandied as a term of political contempt, Campbell used it as the title of a book in which he depicted the many types of an agricultural country, from the farm labourer, the horse breaker and the pig jobber to the whelk gatherer, the herdsman and that new

type created by an Act of Parliament, the old age pensioner. There is grim irony in his depiction of that last sad type:

> For fifty years he trenched his field
> That he might eat a freeman's bread:
> The seasons balked him of his yield,
> His children's children wished him dead.
> But ransom came to him at length
> At the ebb-tide of life and strength.
>
> And so he sits with folded hands
> Over the flag of amber fire:
> He blinks and nods and understands,
> He has his very soul's desire.
> In dew wetted, in tempest blown,
> A Lear at last come to his own.

So our poetry had passed into what we might call the folk phase and many writers, including Pearse, MacDonagh, Alice Milligan, Dora Sigerson, James Stephens, F. R. Higgins were to explore that mode in different ways. In his revolt against the sophisticated refinement of the Celtic Twilight phase, Synge had declared, "It may almost be said that before verse can be human again it must learn to be brutal." But despite his protest, the traditional discipline of the *Love Sagas* which Douglas Hyde had saved from neglect, with all their imaginative idealism, was a prevailing influence and kept these writers from mere violence of words.

Meanwhile our poetry was developing in other directions. While Joyce was meditating over his early realistic stories of Dublin, Seamus O'Sullivan had already discovered for himself the poetic aspect of the city. In subtle rhythms he suggested the lingering Georgian atmosphere of Dublin and evoked in memorable glimpses that eighteenth century to which Yeats was to return later. The aristocratic grandeur of the past, the shabbiness of present-day alley and side-street are contained in lyrics which are all too few in number. A crazy beggar woman sits eating her evening meal on the steps of a Merrion Square mansion, the organ-grinder plays in drab streets, and from the tenements, which were once great houses, the children run to frolic around the ragman or the piper. At dusk through the quiet streets the last lamplighter steals:

> Soundlessly touching one by one
> The waiting posts that stand to take
> The faint blue bubbles in his wake;

And when the night begins to wane
He comes to take them back again,
Before the chilly dawn can blight
The delicate frail buds of light.

O'Sullivan learnt something of his art from the modern French lyric of Samain and de Regnier, and his prose and verse have the same precision. Here are some lines, humorously tantalising in their evasive rhythm, in which the Phoenix Park in sunshine, the lighter history of the British occupation, the daring of the young and the regrets of the old, are all suggested with an unerring touch.

The sunlight shone down on the long road,
    deserted and silent;
No motor, nor cyclist, nor horseman, nor even—
To trouble its peace—a pedestrian,
Save only for me, who went silent,
And a young girl who passed me, demure,
And as fresh as the Spring, and as lovely,
And daintily stepping.
And yet as she passed me I swear to you
    somebody coughed,
No merely civilian, inadequate, meaningless cough.
But a soldier's cough, chesty, profound,
And female-attention-compelling.
Yet the road was quite empty
Save only for me, who went silent,
And the lovely demure-stepping maid,
And the statue of Gough on his horse,
With his field-marshal's baton.

31

The poetry of the city was quickened by the sudden appearance of James Stephens, a poet whose irrepressible, irreverent humour soared above the dire poverty in which his childhood had been spent. His *Insurrections*, published in 1909, was not a political prospectus but a highly individualistic protest against conventional notions. Unequal as they are, these poems of side-streets are full of anger, pity, grotesque fancy. Many were startled by *What Tomas an Buile said in a Pub, Mac Dhoul,* and other somersaults into angelology. But when I read now the animadversions in which some of our younger critics still persist, I recall Thomas MacDonagh's delight in the work of Stephens. He told me how he had lent him the *Epithalamium* of Edmund Spenser, that wonderful marriage song of the Elizabethan poet and political adventurer, and how its joyful refrains had inspired Stephens to daily flights of lyrical fancy. Later James Stephens was to discipline himself by studying Irish, but, characteristically enough, his translations are quick personal re-creations, a hint, a phrase being enough to start his own poetic variations. No doubt, he is a poet of tricks, but he loved little words, brooded over concepts which owe something to A.E., and continued fancifully to sport with time and space.

> The small, green leaf
> Fell down from the tree:
>
> And the great oak tree
> Fell down from the cliff:
>
> And the huge, hard cliff
> Slipped down to the sea:

And the sea was sucked
To the sun in a whiff:

Then . . . blink !
And a shout !

And the sun
Blew out . . .

Owing to the pervasive influence of oral tradition during
those years, our poets tended to write of the poor, the lowly,
the unfortunate. Unlike so many writers of to-day, however,
they were mostly devoid of all social propaganda. But just
as the Celtic Twilight School expressed in its images the half
light and melancholy dusk of our island climate, so these
poets, while avoiding obvious comment, reflected indirectly
the impoversihed state of our country during centuries of
alien rule.

Amid all the stir and excitement of those years the dramatic
movement had been spreading. We lacked an imaginitive
drama such as Schiller and his fellow poets had given to
Germany. But if Yeats had needed an immediate incentive,
there was the contemporary example of Strindberg, who,
in his last years, gave to Sweden, though in prose, a complete
cycle of historical drama. Already in his early plays, *The
Countess Cathleen*, and *The Land of Heart's Desire*, Yeats had
broken away from the Victorian convention of poetic drama
—those long blank-verse plays in five acts, which borrowed
their rhetoric from Shakespearean tragedy. English verse
drama had sunk into decline in the 1840's and had gradually
passed from the stage to the study, so it is not usually realised

that Yeats had to create his own models. He concentrated on short plays, in which every line must have its own poetic quality, sharing the same ideal of perfection with Synge, who held that every speech should be " as fully flavoured as a nut or an apple." As Yeats was essentially lyrical in his genius, his plays have little action, but spoken rightly, they move effectively in their own remote region of imagery and thought, so that we seem brought awhile :

> under the ragged thorns
> That are upon the edge of those great waters
> Where all things vanish away.

Such plays as *The King's Threshold, Deirdre, On Baile's Strand, The Green Helmet*, present the heroic age through his own lyrical temperament and, as late as 1911, he was still perfecting *The Shadowy Waters*, a twilight play, in which all action is resolved into mood and other-worldly desire. Though limited in their appeal, these verse dramas yield us an imaginative experience that is strange and rare. Critics have complained that Yeats failed to give us a powerful, swift-moving drama of the heroic age, but the unforseen is always happening, and instead, he gave us a new kind of play, the lyric drama of the stage. But the poet could not have forseen that the National Theatre which he founded, was to become eventually the very market of our mirth. Looking back, we are tempted to think that the rapid success of the Abbey Theatre in its first formative years was too sensational. The riots over *The Playboy of the Western World*, the naive Kiltartan dialect of Lady Gregory's comedies, the constant tours in England and America, all led to hasty twentieth-century publicity at a time when our growing drama needed careful protection.

34

Abandoning in disappointment the conventions of the stage, Yeats found for himself in the ceremonial *Noh* plays of Japan a new form for his legendary themes. In his Dance Plays, with their elaborate symbols and masks, he was able to combine past and present, range from Irish Mythology to the Rebellion of Easter Week, explore strange gnostic beliefs. His later plays, such as *Purgatory* and *The Herne's Egg,* demand a special audience for they are complex in idea and concentrated in thought. Nevertheless the terse rhythm and speech are powerful in their effect.

IV

The popular tradition of political and patriotic verse was sternly avoided by most of the new writers at the turn of the century, but, curiously enough, it was maintained and given a deeper significance by some women poets. In *Dirge of the Munster Forest* and *Clare Coast*, and other poems, Emily Lawless had evoked with sombre power the seventeenth century, suggesting in terse lines all its tragic historical implications. In 1908 came *Hero Lays* by Alice Milligan, poems with a new, exultant note, that expressed the intense spirit

of nationalism stirring here and there in the country. Here are two stanzas from her *Song of Freedom* :

> On Urris of Inish-Owen,
> As I went up the mountain side,
> The brook that came leaping down
> Cried to me—for joy it cried;
> And when from off the summit far
> I looked o'er land and water wide,
> I was more joyous than the brook
> That met me on the mountain side.
>
> To Ara of Connacht's isles,
> As I went sailing o'er the sea,
> The wind's word, the brook's word,
> The wave's word, was plain to me—
> "As we are, though she is not
> As we are, shall Banba be—
> There is no King can rule the wind,
> There is no fetter for the sea."

In these unequal poems of Alice Milligan, past and present were seen in the same heroic light: Cuchulain, Brian of the Tributes, the revolutionaries and exiles of the Fenian Rising, forgotten in their defeat, the language revivalists—all had their part in the successive epic of struggle.

When we turn, however, to the poets who were to lead the Easter Rising of 1916, we find that they were concerned with the literary problems of the time rather than with political propaganda. Influenced by the elder writers, they were exploring for themselves mythology, oral tradition and Gaelic literature. Padraic Pearse wrote his short stories and plays

37

in Irish: the saga of Cuchulain and the religious songs of Connacht being his main inspiration. His poems, both in Irish and English were few, but the best of them are remarkable for what might be called their prophetic note. Thomas MacDonagh translated literally some of the brief intense poems which Pearse wrote in simple Irish:

> I turned my back
>   On the dream I had shaped,
> And to this road before me
>   My face I turned.

> I set my face
>   To the road here before me,
> To the work that I see,
>   To the death that I shall get.

While Pearse was content with monologue, his companion poets, Joseph Plunket and Thomas MacDonagh were attempting to find a more complex form for religious poetry. In order to avoid the powerful influence of Francis Thompson and other English Catholic poets, they turned to the Spanish mystics. There is little doubt, however, that their interest was stimulated also by the pervasive influence of A.E. for mysticism had almost become an intrinsic part of the movement and these young poets were endeavouring to form a Christian school of thought. But their first experiments were only tentative, and Plunkett's well-known poem, *I see His Blood upon the Rose*, was unconsciously influenced by a lyrical passage from one of the later narratives of Tennyson. As a poet MacDonagh had developed slowly and, in order to school himself, he turned to translation. He drew attention to a distinctive form of lyrical monologue found in medieval Gaelic poetry, a form which, I think, influenced Pearse. MacDonagh's version of the monologue of Eve, " Great Adam's Wife," has the compactness of the original.

> I a kingly house forsook:
> Ill my choise and my disgrace:
> Ill the counsel that I took,
> Withering me and all my race.
>
> I that brought the Winter in,
> And the windy, glistening sky:
> I that brought terror and sin,
> Hell and pain, and sorrow, I.

His critical study, *Literature in Ireland,* was the first sustained attempt to define the aim and nature of an independent literature in this country, and the book was only completed shortly before his death.

The execution of Pearse, MacDonagh and Plunkett by the British military had a profound effect on our other poets and stirred in some of them that impassioned eloquence which had been avoided for so long. Yeats, in two poems which have become famous, A.E., Lady Gregory, Seumas O'Sullivan, Padraic Colum, James Stephens, Joseph Campbell, were among those who protested. Joseph Campbell's *Raven's Rock,* is an historical *Aisling,* or vision of revolt throughout the ages, ending with the fate of Roger Casement.

> I go to the rope and the quicklime,
> They have no hands that would deliver me—
> O, Christ of Nazareth, no hands !

On one of the battlefields abroad, Francis Ledwidge wrote several elegies which have a peculiar poignancy for he was killed a few weeks later in what he had come to regard as an alien cause. The poetry of this young Meath writer had a rare quality of its own and his death at an early age was another loss to the literature of a small country. His nature lyrics were full of delightful images of fancy. Here are some lines from his poem, *A Twilight in Middle March*.

> Within the oak a throb of pigeon wings
> Fell silent and grey twilight hushed the fold,
> And spiders' hammocks swung on half-oped things
> That shook like foreigners upon our cold.
>
> A gipsy made a fire and made a sound
> Of moving tins, and from an oblong moon
> The river seemed to gush across the ground
> To the cracked metre of a marching tune.

He speaks of an old field gate ' swinging upon the wind the anvil song,' and whenever I see the crescent moon with a star near its tip, I remember how he compared it quaintly with ' the cuckoo and her little mother.'

The troubled excited years after the Rebellion saw the rise of a powerful realistic prose, political, angry, topical, and contrary to the deeper emotional mood of our poetry. Shortly after the Rebellion, Eimar O'Duffy, a brilliant novelist, who died young, criticised violently the revolutionary movement in his book, *The Wasted Island,* and satirised the poetic mysticism of MacDonagh and Plunkett. He anticipated the coming acerbity, for the strain of idealism had been too much for a country in search of prosperity and the emotional reaction too disturbing. The atrocities of the Black and Tan period, the founding of the Free State, the shock and humiliation of the Civil War, were reflected immediately in novels, plays and stories, which were as exciting and embittered as the events they depicted. Joyce, in his exile, remained aloof, but the realistic movement with its demand for complete freedom of expression, for which he had laboured as consistently as any political extremist, had reached this country in full strength. Naturalism had, of course, caused a *furore* in France and other countries in the nineteenth century, but in Ireland it seemed new and conflicted at once with popular opinion. Novelists and playwrights began to explore the national character at a time when the nation, itself, in the first experimental years of self-government, was discovering again its own acquisitiveness. Realism, with its outspokenness, its persistent enquiry, sincere, or merely sensational, was regarded as obnoxious. To combat such displeasing mental activity our statesmen reverted to the political methods of the physical force movement. In effect literary realism was proscribed by the Censorship Act and most of our prose writers are on the condemned list. Poetry, slow, opposed to rhetoric, needing time for pondering, and deeper in its imaginative implications than prose, could not compete with all this lively writing which excited so much attention abroad partly because of its apt topicality. Traditional and essentially romantic, it did not seek to chastise, but could use later the more subtle methods of sorrowful irony.

V

The first World War and the age-old emotions stirred in our country by the Rebellion gave for a time another significance to our mythology. Those Asiatic stories, changing as they moved westward through obscure centuries, seemed to adum-brate the forces stirring so violently again in the human race. My own early poems were of an epic kind for I had been influenced by Ferguson and Herbert Trench, and it seemed to me that only in a remote way could the primitive forces still in civilisation be expressed. Life itself was an epic struggle, for I had spent my childhood resisting the mightiest of fallen angels, intent on seizing my small soul. Youth itself, though a transitory possession, seemed as valuable for the Great Powers of the militant world demanded it from the new generation everywhere. In the *Toruigheacht Dhiarmuda agus Ghráinne* I found what I wanted, for this Gaelic pursuit-tale is about two young lovers who fled from violence, night and day, through the glens and forests of Ireland, wishing only to be happy and to be left alone. Later I wrote of the cattle war which was the start of the Cuchulain epic, for great miserable droves from the cattle market of Dublin passed our garden gate every Thursday on their way to slaughter in England and affected me in dreams.

My contemporary, F. R. Higgins, was delighting in the *Love Songs of Connaught,* but new aspects of our literature were already before us. In his book, *The Hidden Ireland,* Daniel Corkery had applied for the first time the standards of literary criticism to Gaelic literature and revealed clearly for us the last poetry of the seventeenth and eighteenth centuries. In the poems of O Bruadair, O Rathaille, Ferriter and others, medieval allegory had survived, blending curiously with classical allusion. The mode of the *Aisling* or Vision poem tempted us to experiment in forgotten forms, for we had revolted against the inordinate claims of nineteenth century symbolism. A.E. kept reminding us constantly of William Larminie's theory, set down in the early 'nineties, that Gaelic assonance could be used in English to modulate rhyme. We listened carelessly and, in my own case, it was not until I met Paul Fort in Paris and studied his use of submerged rhyme that the experiment seemed to me possible. The assonantal patterns of Gaelic prosody are intricate, but in the simplest form the tonic word at the end of the line is supported by an assonance in the middle of the next line. The use of such patterns in English is limited but they can change the pivotal movement of the lyric stanza. In some forms of early syllabic Gaelic metres, only one part of a double-syllable word is used in assonance, a system also found in the Spanish ballad metres, and this suggested experiment in partial rhyming and muting. For example, we can have rhyme or assonance, on or off accent, stopped rhyme, (e.g. ring, kingdom; breath, method), harmonic rhyme (e.g. hero, window), cross-rhyme.

In illustration I venture to give some examples of my own experiments. Here is an example of a fairly strict pattern from a paraphrase of a Gaelic poem:

> Summer delights the scholar
>   With knowledge and reason:
> Who is happy in hedgerow
>   Or meadow as he is?

Paying no dues to the parish,
    He argues in logic
And has no care of cattle
    But a satchel and stick.

The showery air grows softer,
    He profits by his ploughland,
For the share of the schoolmen
    Is a pen in hand . . .

Here are two stanzas from an *Aisling* or vision poem, in
which stopped rhyme is used:

Coil of her hair, in cluster and ringlet,
Had brightened round her forehead and those curls—
Closer than she could bind them on a finger—
Were changing gleam and glitter. O she turned
So gracefully aside, I thought her clothes
Were flame and shadow while she slowly walked,
Or that each breast was proud because it rode
The cold air as the wave stayed by the swan.

But knowing her face was fairer than in thought,
I asked of her was she the Geraldine—
Few horsemen sheltered at the steps of water?
Or that Greek woman, lying in a piled room
On tousled purple, whom the household saved,
When frescoes of strange fire concealed the pillar:
The white coin all could spend? Might it be Niav
And was she over wave or from our hills?

Lastly a more varied use in some lines from a later poem:

> Morning has moved the dreadful candle,
> Appointed shadows cross the nave;
> Unlocked by the secular hand,
> The very elements remain
> Appearances upon the altar.
> Adoring priest has turned his back
> Of gold upon the congregation.
> All saints have had their day at last,
> But thought still lives in pain.
>
> How many councils and decrees
> Have perished in the simple prayer
> That gave obedience to the knee;
> Trampling of rostrum, feathering
> Of pens at cock-rise, sum of reason
> To elevate a common soul:
> Forgotten as the minds that bled
> For us, the miracle that raised
> A language from the dead . . .

The Celtic-Romanesque era with its intricate patterns in verse, in stone, metal and illumination, its conventionalised impersonal forms, attracted us as objective writers in an age of self-dramatisation and display. Further technical experiment in a different direction was made by F. R. Higgins. Undisturbed by prose realism, he did not swerve from the lyrical strain found in the *Love Songs* and for some years he lived near Mount Nephin in the west. In the tune rhythms of Irish traditional music he found patterns for his lyrics, matching word and note, and this accounts for his addiction to the vocative case. But by subtle variation he endeavoured to

suggest " the gapped music " of an ancient scale. His experi-
ments were too fine to gain immediate appreciation because
many ears have been coarsened, but the late W. J. Turner,
distinguished poet and music critic, endeavoured to draw
attention to them. Here is the first stanza of a lyric by F. R.
Higgins entitled *The Three-Cornered Field* :

> By a field of the crab-tree my love and I were walking
> And talking most sweetly to each other;
> In the three-cornered field, O we walked in early autumn,
> And these were the words of my lover.

As W. J. Turner points out, the lines are written to a simple
folk-tune and most readers will be able to realise that fact
without knowing any particular melody, but only the rhythmic
pattern is there and the use of end-assonance has the same
effect as diminished intervals in music. Subtlety in tune rhythm
could scarcely have been carried further than in this lyric :

> When pails empty the last brightness
> Of the well, at twilight-time,
> And you are there, among women—
> O, mouth of silence,
> Will you come with me, when I sign,
> To the far green wood, that fences
> A lake inlaid with light ?
>
> To be there, O, lost in each other,
> While day melts in airy water,
> And the drake-headed pike—a shade
> In the waves' pale stir !
> For love is there, under the breath,
> As a coy star is there in the quiet
> Of the wood's blue eye.

In speech rhythm, too, F. R. Higgins was achieving rare skill before his premature death. Here are some lines that have the movement of living speech and yet avoid the lack of tension to be found in so much free verse:

> Only last week, walking the hushed fields
> Of our most lovely Meath, now thinned by November,
> I came to where the road from Laracor leads
> To the Boyne river—that seemed more lake than river,
> Stretched in uneasy light and stript of reeds . . .

VI

George Moore has given us in that diverting trilogy of his, *Hail and Farewell*, a consecutive legend of the literary movement in Dublin before the first great war. Life itself is rarely as consecutive as legend, and so we may suspect that he was really bored at times and in his mocking pages invented many an exhilarating scene in order to while away the long summer evenings in town. But when I was a student he seemed to me the chronicler of great days that had just gone. The dominating figure was still W. B. Yeats and truly his renown was a visible legend. He had patrons, a theatre of his own, a private press and publishers ready to reprint the everchanging versions of his plays and poems. Young poets stared through the windows of the Dublin bookshops and saw his volumes displayed in them, with covers that were a blaze of gold, that gold which had been used so profusely in the 'nineties to adorn the Book Beautiful. In the art shops his best known lyrics—such as *The Lake Isle of Innisfree*, and *When you are old and grey and full of sleep*—all hand-printed, illustrated and framed, were on sale; and we saw those framed poems hung on the drawing-room walls of every house with any pretensions to good taste. We were puzzled and excited by the paradox of it all. This poet, whose lyrics brought us, as by an instant spell, into shadowy Celtic regions where only the reeds murmured, this companion of elemental spirits and fairy-folk, was an active public figure. He had lectured in England and throughout the United States many times, founded Irish literary societies, engaged in sensational controversies, and was unsparing of his very presence. Whenever a play of his was performed at the Abbey Theatre before the customary farce, he appeared on the top of the steps leading down to the auditorium as the last gong sounded and house lights were dimmed, a mysterious twilight figure. When his play ended, he appeared just as mysteriously on the stage, a long black lock falling over his forehead as he waved his arms rhythmically and spoke to us in a voice that was half a chant.

The unexpected is always happening and few could have foretold then that Yeats would return to the ample manner of the past, revive it for himself and enrich it with his own musical cadences. The entire movement had been a revolt against that tradition and, with the decline of the Irish Parliamentary Party and the rise of Sinn Fein, the age of speech-making had passed. Poetic eloquence is, of course, quite distinct from oratory, but public poet and orator have this in common: they see all largely, estimate all in terms of historical importance. Yeats showed admirable courage in turning to that dignified mode in a period of change and, curiously enough, it proved popular, not so much here as in England and America. Modernists affect to think little of all that Yeats wrote before the age of fifty, but they welcomed the sombre magnificence of his later mood, finding in it perhaps an escape from the deliberate drabness of their own productions. Regarding his work as a whole, however, we may suspect that Yeats never really left the Celtic Twilight. For all its questioning and excited enquiry, its schematic arrangement of opposites, his later poetry celebrates mourn-fully the passing of greatness. In his ranging themes he sums up an era and for us his language seems to bring to a poetic and glorious end the tradition of Anglo-Irish eloquence, for it has the vibrant timbre which can be heard in Burke's prose when he recalls his memories of Marie Antoinette and in that last speech made by Grattan in the Irish House of Commons before the Act of Union. He evokes memories of his dead friends, and their shades mingle with the ghosts and spirits of folklore and of the séances which were a vogue in the nineteenth century. The modernists, by their interest, undoubtedly stimulated Yeats and gave perhaps a mischievous zest to the speculation of his old age. Had his earlier reputation not been assailed by them, he might have been content to settle down as a dignified, stately figure—in his own words, "a smiling public man." But he was resolved in his own way to comment on the poetic din across the sea.

> ' The fiddlers are all thumbs,
> Or the fiddle-string accursed,
> The drum and the kettledrums
> And the trumpets are all burst,
> And the trombone,' cried he,
> The trumpet and the trombone,'
> And cocked a malicious eye,
> ' But time runs on, runs on.'

He turned to philosophical speculation but treated it all imaginatively, becoming extravagant as Seanchan in his own play, *The King's Threshold.*

> For when the body has grown weak,
> There's nothing that can tether the wild mind
> That, being moonstruck and fantastical,
> Goes where it fancies.

He drew increasingly upon the immense amount of pedantic occult lore, astrology and marvels with which he had excited his imagination throughout a lifetime. In England and America the oddest, the most fantastic speculation cannot alarm, but in Ireland, where strict conformity of mind has been customary for ages, such speculation is provocative. In effect, Yeats was really cocking a malicious eye at us.

The religious art of the Celtic-Romanesque period is derived from Byzantium and, to know the origins of our thought, we must return to that city in which the first Christian dogmas were shaped. It is significant, however, that in his two poems on Byzantium, poems which have become famous, Yeats did not express the emergence of a spiritual order. With superb imagery taken from mosaic and goldwork, the odes gather into themselves the extravagance of semi-oriental fable, and in them the poet defines his own doctrine of art as a balance of contraries.

> Astraddle on the dolphin's mire and blood,
> Spirit after spirit! The smithies break the flood,
> The golden smithies of the Emperor!
> Marbles of the dancing floor

Break bitter furies of complexity,
Those images that yet
Fresh images beget,
That dolphin-torn, that gong-tormented sea.

In the poems which Yeats wrote during his old age there
is yet another change, for he returned in memory to that
poorer Ireland which he had known in his childhood.
Crazy Jane, Jack the Journeyman, Tom the Lunatic—these
tatterdemalions of his mind might have been the last victims
of the Famine or fit troop for King Lear in his dotage. The
poet expresses through them an abandonment that is true
to folk lore in its wilder moments, an apparent despair that
is really exhilaration, and reading such a lyric as the following,
we forget that he had little Latin and less Greek.

Bolt and bar the shutter,
For the foul winds blow:
Our minds are at their best this night,
And I seem to know
That everything outside us is
Mad as the mist and snow.

Horace there by Homer stands,
Plato stands below,
And here is Tully's open page.
How many years ago
Were you and I unlettered lads
Mad as the mist and snow?

You ask what makes me sigh, old friend,
What makes me shudder so?
I shudder and I sigh to think
That even Cicero
And many-minded Homer were
Mad as the mist and snow.

VII

Although Ireland can conceal its immense age at times,
our poets are not deceived and so some of them feel the need
to escape from the responsibilities which are so often our
impediment. In this small island there is, as Yeats wrote,
'little room,' and it was a feeling of constriction which made
him turn to Milton, Dryden and Landor in his later years.
But even in the early days of the movement, when the recovery
of tradition was still novel, there were poets who refused
to meddle in what seemed strange matters. Oliver St. John
Gogarty, for example, kept steadfastly to the classical tradition,
though, curiously enough, he derived his technique from
the *Lays of Ancient Rome*. Yet he had a precedent, for Macaulay,
that master of the active verb, had inspired Thomas Davis
and the political poets of the early nineteenth century. His gift
for the epigrammatic phrase is shown in that well-known
poem of his, *Non Dolet*.

Then do not shudder at the knife
That Death's indifferent hand drives home;
But with the Strivers leave the Strife,
Nor, after Caesar, sulk in Rome.

Captain T. M. Kettle, who was killed in France during the first world war, had satiric wit. There is deep feeling, however, in his memorable lines:

> Know that we fools, now with the foolish dead,
> Died not for flag, nor King, nor Emperor,
> But for a dream, born in a herdsman's shed,
> And for the secret Scripture of the poor.

D. L. Kelleher lived abroad for many years, but has written a dramatic sequence of poems about Cork city. The emotional dilemma has been expressed by Monk Gibbon, an accomplished poet and one of our few essayists:

> No land sees me now
> Five moons or longer,
> Even she who reared
> Proves little stronger.
> I have lost her speech;
>
> Her men would count me
> Stranger if I spoke,
> Not of their country.
> I have lost her ways,
> Her thought, her murmur;
> I have lost all
> But my love for her.

But this dilemma is wider than poetry and has always been shown in the conflicting tendencies of the country itself; the divergence has been intensified since we are now enduring the painful and pleasant experiments of independence. It is shown in the desire to conserve our tradition and develop the Irish language again, and in the equally powerful desire to industrialise ourselves, dam our rivers for energy, burn up our bogs as fast as we can, and merge ourselves with the twentieth century.

During recent years the struggle between separate culture and international standardisation, which has been carried on elsewhere, can be seen here on a smaller scale. An anthology of recent Irish verse edited by two young poets, Valentin Iremonger and Robert Greacen and published by Faber and Faber, shows how strong has been the influence of modernism during the last decade or so. Unfortunately, the book contains no preface and, as our younger writers have not issued any statement of their aims, it is difficult to estimate completely their intentions. It is important, however, to distinguish between the two aims of recent poetry. The first is artistic, the attempt to intensify the medium and to express in it complex moods and ideas; the second is to make poetry utilitarian by using the general vocabulary and rhythms of prose, and by discussing in it topics of political, social and economic interest. Few of our younger writers, however, seem interested in industrialisation and only Ewart Milne and Leslie Daiken deal with questions of social reform. Denis Devlin writes strictly in the intellectual manner of modern French poets and this obscures his satiric impulse. The title of two books by Blanaid Salkeld may be taken to signify the fact that our experimentalists are conservative in thought, for if *the engine is left running* indicates a desire for earthly speed, *Hello, Eternity !* suggests an enviable familiarity with a happier world than this one. Among those who have passed without too much affliction through the prosaic phase of experiment is Donagh

MacDonagh, who wrote recently a highly successful verse comedy of Dublin life, *Happy as Larry*. Geoffrey Taylor explores neglected byways of nineteenth century Ireland; Maurice Craig has turned towards the eighteenth century, and Patrick MacDonogh has followed partly the lyrical mode of F. R. Higgins. Our women writers have in general avoided the discontents of our time. Winifred Letts is a well-known writer and, among others, may be mentioned Mary Devenport O'Neill, Sheila Wingfield, Temple Lane, Rhoda Coghill. Translation from Gaelic poetry has increased in recent years and this useful literary drill is due, no doubt, to the spreading knowledge of the language. Our best-known translators are Frank O'Connor, Arland Ussher, Aodh de Blacam and the Earl of Longford.

The problem and plight of our poetry to-day can be indicated if we turn to the work of John Lyle Donaghy who died recently. All his poetry appeared in private editions and the lack even of a small public was, I think, a loss to him for, with the years, it increased that strain of pedantry which is not unpleasing in his early lyrics. He was influenced at first by the sparse style of Joseph Campbell, and I find in those clear-toned early lyrics of his, known to so few, a constant delight. Here is one of them entitled *Glenarm* :

> Past ploughed and fallow, at the top
> Of the glen where stunted hazels grow,
> With pensive show
> Of white moss-banded arms that drop,
> Wind-struck, into the daisy crop;
> There, on a thought, the first doe would rise
> With daisy meads in her two eyes.

Past forest bridge and up the slope
Where slim and straight the hazels grow,
But closer now,
Ringstraked with light and all a⁄drop
With dazzling mist until you stop;
There, at a sound, the last stag would rise
With hazel woods in his two eyes.

Let me quote a few lines from another poem of his about the Scottish Highlands entitled *Winter*.

The feathery forests are blown back, frost rends
    The mountain⁄spar and moulds
The thrift leaf where the lean wild cat descends
    Out of his Grampian holds;
The wild white goat forsakes the clamorous height,
    In the half dawn comes down
And rears his horns against the lily light
    And bleats out through the town;
The redwing leaves the Scandinavian skies
    And snowflowers fallen by night
Through his black cover⁄twigs and cross⁄sea hies
    With long untwittering flight.

Influenced by contemporary practice, Lyle Donaghy turned to free verse and he is the only one of our writers who has experimented consistently in that form. His rhythmical effects are remarkable but they are attained, I think, at too great a cost. The longer rhythms of free verse seem to necessitate the use of larger words and so this difficult medium can lead to a heavily latinised vocabulary. It is significant that Lyle Donaghy turned eventually to the study of Irish, feeling the

need of another discipline. R. N. D. Wilson, another of
our poets, has written rich graceful lyrics, such as *Saint
Apollinare in Classe*

> Thought swarmed here once; the stark
> Thebaid brake its comb,
> and poured out of the dark
> wild honey to Rome.

His skill in free measures can be seen in *Elegy in a Presbyterian
Burying-Ground*, a moving tribute to his friend, Lyle Donaghy,
from which I quote the third stanza:

> Son of the manse he was,
> And drew his integrity from these whitewalled precincts,
> His rhetoric from his father's pulpit phrase.
> Though he himself had made his Covenant elsewhere,
> An older, darker and more troubled one,
> With the certainty of a leaf, of a stone, of a dewdrop,
> He knew his Election.

And here is the concluding stanza:

> Yet he would grieve with me for the dereliction
> That has overtaken this place,
> Since he cared for it. And the burying-ground beside it
> Held many of his race.
> He would not be surprised to find it sadly neglected,
> Who was himself so negligent of fame.
> And I?
> —I would be proud to be the stoneyard mason
> Who had incised his name.

It is too soon to judge the effect of the modernistic influence here with its mood of disillusion, but the same discontent can be found in our novels and plays, and so verse can hardly escape. For example, we find that discontent struggling against itself in the poetry of Patrick Kavanagh and the fact that his output is so small is probably due in part to confusion of purpose. At the age of thirty-three, he appeared as ploughman-poet with a pamphlet of simple verse and an unusual autobiography in prose entitled *The Green Fool*. The book was idyllic, for the writer was determined to find poetry in straws, and he tells us that from the onion box which had been converted into a cradle for him he saw the sky first through holes that the blackbirds had pecked in the thatch. He had the courage to react from this conventional cult of the wonderful peasant and published, some years later, a collection of frank poems. In contrast with some wistful memories of childhood, there is a remarkable long poem entitled *The Great Hunger*, realistic in design. It is written in rough free verse but the very roughness suits the mood of disillusion—and the blackbirds have gone.

> Here crows gabble over worms and frogs
> And the gulls like old newspapers are blown
> clear of the hedges.

The note of squalor is increased by contrast—

> Primroses and the unearthly start of ferns
> Among the blackthorn shadows in the ditch,
> A dead sparrow and an old waistcoat.

Life in the countryside has become a depressing routine of misery, solitary temptation in small fields, repression, late marriage.

> Watch him, watch him, that man on a hill whose spirit
> Is a wet sack flapping about the knees of time.

Avoiding the lyric mood, the poet relies on direct statement and the total effect of drabness is powerful. Sharing the impatience of our realistic novelists, Patrick Kavanagh expresses that tedium and discontent which have helped to increase the flight from the land and the crowding into cities.

In a vigorous poem entitled *Pegasus,* he presents the poet of to-day as a displaced person.

> Where the
> Tinkers quarrel I went down
> With my horse, my soul.
> I cried, ' Who will bid me half a crown ? '
> From their rowdy bargaining
> No one turned. ' Soul,' I prayed,
> ' I have hawked you through the world
> Of Church and State and meanest trade.
> But this evening, halter off,
> Never again will it go on.
> On the south side of ditches
> There is grazing of the sun.
> No more haggling with the world . . . '

Despite partition, the immediate problems of our poetry are similar in Northern Ireland. Louis MacNeice achieved rapidly a reputation as one of the leaders of the English advanced group which was so active in the years before the last war, and W. R. Rodgers, who has a remarkable gift for imagery, is generally regarded as belonging to the same school, but his early poems are Irish in subject and, like other wanderers, he may return to us. Of the poets who have remained in Ulster, Roy MacFadden and John Hewitt may be mentioned. The latter is as yet a solitary " regionalist," and has found inspiration in the Ulster country, side, the neglected ballads and lore of the Planter tradition.

VIII

This is still an ecclesiastical country, though anchorites can no longer be found in cave or on remote Atlantic rock. It is inevitable, therefore, the we should be drawn towards the next world, but some of us believe that religious verse must be analytic now and we remember at midnight that axiom of Ibsen—

> Poetry—'tis a Court
> Of Judgment on the soul.

However, our younger religious poets would scarcely agree with us. Robert Farren is not a visionary or mystic, despite the titles of his early volumes of verse, *Thronging Feet*, and *Time's Wall Asunder*. He is a poet of doctrine, much pleased by all that has been defined for us and his first task has been ambitious, for he attempted to free us from the encroaching tradition of the English convert school and find his own means of expression. He has written a book of short stories in Irish, and it was, no doubt, his knowledge of our early literature and the increasing interest in our long neglected mediaeval heritage that sent him to a subject which gave him space, distance and objectivity. In his long lyric-epic poem, *The First Exile*, published in 1944, his imagination escaped into the semi-druidic cycle of legends that surround the life of St. Colmcille, but, stricter than a hagiologist, he disciplined the theme for himself. His poem, in its originality, causes mental resistance at a first encounter, for one feels in it the clashing enthusiasm of a new bi-lingualism. Like our elder poets in the joy of re-discovery, he dotes on Gaelic words, and so they are swept into his narrative. He will have ' bawn ' for ' meadow ' and, with more excuse, ' ceannavaun ' for ' bog-cotton.'

> Over the bawns of water they hove to the northward,
> bawns full of johnswort gold and blue of clovers
> under the sun going down; and over the greening
> and grey-growing bawns of water in dews and hazes;
> and over the ceannavaun moors of the waters in
> moon-ray—
> stroking, and stroking, and stroking the boats
> through the ocean.
>
> Till the sky moved its light like the hues of a
> shell turned slowly,
> and morning hove out with a shiver and a sparkle
> on the waters,
> and the droning of the sea was chinked-through
> with the squealing of the gannets.

The story tells how Colmcille went into exile in order to mortify his terrible temper, and settled in Iona. The changing measures move swiftly, energetically, while end assonance, half rhyme and rhyme hurry past. The chosen words are hard, tense, consonantal, for Robert Farren is perhaps our first poet to draw on the systematised alliteration of Gaelic verse. His language compels us to realise that these monks of Colmcille are makers of things, strugglers against substance: they forge, dig, tan, knock carefully together. So we have the bell maker—

> I make the bells
> in the fog of the foundry,
> thick fire on my gills,
> soot and cinder around me,
> with clawtongs and anvil
> and sledge and handhammer
> flint troughs of chill water
> hot bronze and brass copper.
> *I make the bells O I make all the bells.*

and here is the slow mason:

> I have mastered the grain, the make, the temper of
>   stone,
> fingering it and considering, touching with hand and
>   with soul,
> quarrying it out of the course, piercing and severing it,
> with a chirp of meeting metals like a bird's chirp.
>
> Basalt I know—bottle green still pools of stone
> harder than hawk's beak, shark's tooth or tusk of
>   the boar;
> basalt—the glass stone, stone without pore or wart;
> causeway stone stepped across Moyle fjord in the north.

62

Granite I know—dust pearl with silver eyes—
that moulds domed hills, with snows, rain, wind and
    time.
Marble—the multiple tinted—the satin flesh—
daughter of the King of white Greece in the lands
    of the west.

Dark flint I know with the feel of a fox's tongue,
the unconsumed cold carrier of fire its young,
stone of hairedges and thornpoints, the dagger stone,
spearstone, swordstone, hatchet stone, hearth gilly stone.

O Christ, the stone which the builders rejected
and which is become the head of the corner,
part me from them the stone shall grind when it fall;
leave me not a stone in thine enemies' hand !

The story culminates around the famous Assembly at Druim
Ceat, to which Colmcille returns from Scotland, to plead
for the poets and prevent their dispersion, a legend which
adumbrates the clash between professional paganism and the
closer organisation of Christianity. In presenting the case
for the poets, Robert Farren draws on the humorous,
imaginative extravagance to be found in the bardic tales,
but we are never in doubt of the issue for the poet is a man
of faith, and so, even in legend, the supremacy of Colmcille
in all ways, lay and ecclesiastical, is ordained before the
very conception of the saint.

  In some of the complimentary love poems which Raftery,
the last of the professional Gaelic poets, made among the
people, that strain of humorous extravagance which was so
constant in our earlier literature reappears. Padraic Fallon,

who comes from the Raftery country in the west, has developed this strain in his adaptations of the Gaelic poet and, like a composer taking a folk tune, he elaborates his own variations.

> For Mary Hynes, rising, gathers up there
> Her ripening body from all the love stories;
> And, rinsing herself at morning, shakes her hair
> And stirs the old gay books in libraries;
> And what shall I do with sweet Boccaccio?
> And shall I send Ovid back to school again
> With a new headline for his copybook,
> And a new pain?

Padraic Fallon is a poet with a strong mythopœic impulse, too impressionable as yet, but with an exciting figurative speech, frenzied at times by modernistic example. But in a poem, such as *Out of Soundings,* he can distinguish between western loquacity and its opposite on the east coast. His ancient mariners in a ship-forgotten port of the south east, deep-water men who have sailed around this astonishing globe, have shut mind and mouth—and so the poet must chase his own albatrosses.

> If their flesh were accurate, they would sweat
> Oceans in bold blue bruises, their heads
> Would glitter like mercury and glass, and I
> Could take the sun as in a sextant
> From each blazing eye,
> And guess the whole wild atlas with its blues
> and reds
> Eere they leave it, useless in the linen, on their
> last bedsteads.

.　　.　　.　　.

I search down their innocent stares.
And they say good morning, or yes the wind will
    rise;
I catch at their minds and they hang limp
In my fingers as empty coat-collars,
Or disgorge with a dry hard rattle simple
And wooden replies
Like toy ships for schoolboys.

And never, though I cherished them, have I
    sensed on some bared nerve,
Dim as in an old green bottle, miraculously
A skyline surge with a great ship—
And had six old men around me in a surf
Of raving radiance striking hip
And thigh for words to make me see
A god by proxy . . .

IX

When Belgium, which is bilingual, became an independent state in 1831, all serious writing, both in French and Flemish, practically disappeared for several generations, but this cannot be quite said of us. Undoubtledly our standards have been affected by the confusion of the times and we have been discovered by the magnates. Our novelists and prose dramatists have been drawn into the competitive market and, though there are honourable exceptions, some of the best of them have become salesmen. The comic brogue of the past has been revived and vies with a purpurate brogue for which we cannot blame Synge. But verse is no longer worth a bad penny and so escapes too much attention. Unfortunately, we have no large publishers here to spend some of their profits on us and we must be content to seek patiently elsewhere. Apart from that, our lucrative printers respect the tradition of their trade which, to some extent, began in eighteenth century 'piracy.' Who can blame them if they find in skull and cross-bones the pious emblems of mortality? But considering that this is a small agricultural country, sparsely populated, we cannot complain overmuch if poetry must depend again on word of mouth. Certainly our poets do not commit suicide in despair as in the United States; nor squabble among themselves so often and so irritably as those in England. I am told that poetry is rarely heard on the American broadcasting system, but here Radio Eireann helps, by regular broadcasts, to spread a knowledge of poetry in general, and only trained verse speakers are used. The British

Broadcasting Corporation, as Mr. Clive Sansom has pointed out in a recent essay, employs actors for most of its readings. " While a few of them are able to adjust their technique and intelligence to lyric poetry, the majority dramatise and declaim it with little feeling for its mood and form. This insensitiveness to poetry is one of the mysteries of broadcasting."

The Lyric Company, founded to save from neglect the tradition of verse drama left to us by Yeats gave special performances regularly in the poet's own theatre for ten years. The enterprise was completely fundless, but owed much to the generosity of actors trained in rhythmic speech and to producers. Plays and dramatic poems by writers of various countries were presented, and among Irish names may be mentioned Yeats, Hyde, Colum, Campbell, Fitzmaurice, Donagh MacDonagh, Mary Devenport O'Neill, Padraic Fallon and my own. In these scant days poetry must be content to go without. Hope may be a foundling but we cannot conceal its birth.

During the last ten years the circumstances of poetry have been changing rapidly. In the United States the poets have retreated from the troublous world into the academic security of numerous small universities. At the same time, owing to American cultural expansion, their books of poems and critical studies are subsidised and, as often as not, are published simultaneously in their own country and in England. So, owing to interchange and rapid communication, British and American poetry have drawn closer together. Anglo-American anthologies of verse, ranging from Chaucer and Shakespeare to the present day, have now become frequent. The merging of old and new tradition should have interesting results.

We have no such deliberate alliance; nevertheless the

present tendency of verse to become subjective is noticeable here as elsewhere. In 1958, at the age of seventy-five, the late Blanaid Salkeld published *Experiment in Error,* having just recovered, as she noted, from " a spell of sonneteering." Taking advantage of the modern freedom of the sonnet, she used the Petrarchan form as a highly individual medium for every mood, direct, conversational, remote, immediate. In the sextet she adopted a rhyme arrangement which is uncommon but very effective: the first and last lines are rhymed and make a frame. In these poems, clear, yet searching, the experience of a life-time is expressed in intellectual and spiritual paradox. Illness and monotony had not silenced this poet, so intent on blending the homely and surprising image, matching confidence with reserve.

> I am become tired warder of the days:
> Each greets me, risen, with a sulphur glare,
> Since I prolong time's wrong, time's useless care—
> The dry routine—though I am loth to raise
> Dead eyes to window, nor can ever praise
> The grudging slave that peddles my despair
> About the parish. I uptie my hair,
> And jolt the jolly mirror with my face,
> Then patter in and out of airless rooms;
> Trip stairs; slam door; and stamp along the street,
> Slapping the solid reticence of day.
> To-morrow forgotten, in the often gay
> Visit of night, I thankfully retreat
> Into a gloomy hazard, like the tomb's.

Concern with social reform and public affairs has dwindled but can be found in the work of Ewart Milne, the late Patrick

MacDonogh, who developed for himself a subtle method of ironic comment, and also in my own recent work which is inspired by belief in the immediate needs for an Irish Welfare State. Among younger poets, Patrick Galvin deals with political and social problems but his allegorical ballads are as yet, I think, much too excitable.

Thomas Kinsella is a new writer who has published three volumes which are remarkable for their variety and range. He is mainly introspective and at times obscure, especially when he uses the analytic method and abstract diction of our time. But he has unexpected lyric moods, as in his poems, *A Lady of Quality* and *Mid-Summer*. A glimpse of our past in the following poem from *Moralities* shows his power of swiftness.

> Grim Deirdre sought the stony fist, her grief
> Capped at last by insult. Pierce's bride,
> Sybil Ferriter, fluttered like a leaf
> And fell in courtly love to stain the tide.
> Each for a murdered husband—hanged in silk
> Or speared in harness—threw her body wide,
> And offered treachery a bloody milk;
> Each cast the other's shadow when she died.

Richard Murphy, whose first book, *The Archaeology of Love*, was mainly European in its themes, intellectual in manner, has reverted to a simpler mode and, in his long narrative poem, *The Last Galway Hooker*, describes vividly and romantically the traditional life of fishermen in the west of Ireland. John Montague has given us in his first book terse, laconic impressions of the United States, where he spent a few years as a student. Some of his best poems, however, express the

69

compulsive memories of his childhood in the country. These are realistic, mordant in humour, rebellious in tone. *The Old People* concludes:

> Ancient Ireland indeed ! I was reared by her bedside,
> The rune and the chant, evil eye and averted head,
> Formorian fierceness of family and local feud.
> Gaunt figures of fear and of friendliness,
> For years they trespassed on my dreams,
> Until once, in s standing circle of stones,
> I felt their shadow pass
> Into that dark permanence of ancient forms.

Among other poets of promise may be mentioned Sean O Criadain, and Desmond O'Grady, both of them living and teaching in Rome. Using the colloquial method, they write of the contemporary scene and glare back at early years in Ireland almost as grimly as our realistic novelists. Using the effective device of a persona, Mr. O'Grady, for example, expresses in *Self-Portrait of Reilly as a Young Man* the complex claims of the artist:

> I must be priest-poet-layman to myself.

Such is the predicament of our younger writers. For a contrast, we have *The Poet's Circuit*, which Padraic Colum, the *doyen* of the Irish literary revival, has just published in his eightieth year. He has lived for many years in New York, but now returns regularly on visits to Ireland. In this collection, he has assembled all the poems of Irish traditional life and passing customs which he has written throughout sixty years. Of this memorable work, the Northern poet and critic, John Hewitt, has written: " It is as if the poet had erected this monument, then picked up his tools and gear and had walked away from it, leaving it, in confidence and humility, to time and weather."

This rapid survey needs perhaps for completeness a brief mention of the literary revival in Gaelic. Behind their own Safety-Curtain is a group of writers fully committed to the restoration and imaginative advancement of what is known in popular phrase as "the medium." Moral problems have not as yet perplexed these new novelists and short-story writers, who are experimenting so enthusiastically in a language which has an enormous vocabulary and much frankness. Among its younger prose writers who have a definite artistic standard may be mentioned Séamus Ó Néill, Tarlach Ó hUid and Máirtín Ó Cadhain, a native speaker, whose dialectic extravagances are as puzzling as the synthetic intensities of James Joyce. The progress of verse in the Irish language has been slower but the movement has now three poets of individual gifts and of high promise, Máirtín Ó Direáin, Séan Ó Riordáin, and Máire Mhac an tSaoi, all of them aware of a complex art and tradition which goes back more than a thousand years.

ACKNOWLEDGEMENTS

Thanks are due to the authors, owners of copyrights and publishers of poems quoted in this booklet.

Thomas Moore (1779-1852)

James Clarence Mangan (1803-1849)

Samuel Ferguson (1810-1886)

Aubrey de Vere (1814-1902)

Thomas Davis (1814-1845)

Charles Gavan Duffy (1816-1903)

William Allingham (1824-1889)

Thomas D'Arcy McGee (1825-1849)

Standish Hayes O'Grady (1832-1915)

Emily Lawless (1845-1913)

Standish James O'Grady (1846-1927)

William Larminie (1849-1900)

Lady Gregory (1852-1932)

Katherine Tynan (1861-1931)

Douglas Hyde (1862-1949)

Herbert Trench (1865-1923)

W. B. Yeats (1865-1939)

Dora Sigerson (1866-1918)

Lionel Johnson (1867-1902)

A.E. (George Russell) (1867-1935)

Eva Gore-Booth (1870-1926)

John M. Synge (1871-1909)

Nora Hopper (1871-1906)

James Cousins (1873-1955)

Thomas MacDonagh (1878-1916)

Daniel Corkery (1878-)

Oliver St. John Gogarty (1878-1957)

Lord Dunsany (1878-1957)

Patrick Pearse (1879-1916)

Joseph Campbell (1879-1944)

Alice Milligan (1880-1953)

Seumas O'Sullivan (1880-)

Blanaid Salkeld (1880-1959)

Padraic Colum (1881-)

Winifred Letts (1882-)

James Joyce (1882-1941)

James Stephens (1883-1950)

Joseph Plunkett (1887-1916)

Francis Ledwidge (1891-1917)

D. L. Kelleher (1883-1958)

Aodh de Blacam (1891-1951)

F. R. Higgins (1896-1932)

Monk Gibbon (1896-)

Austin Clarke (1896-)

R. N. D. Wilson (1899-1953)

Arland Ussher (1899-)

Geoffrey Taylor (1900-1956)

Mary Devonport O'Neill (1895-)

Lyle Donaghy (1902-1946)

Patrick MacDonagh (1902-1961)

Lord Longford (1902-1961)

Frank O'Connor (1903-)

Ewart Milne (1903-)

Rhoda Coghill (1903-)

Temple Lane (1899-)

Patrick Kavanagh (1905-)

Padraic Fallon (1906-)

Louis MacNeice (1907-)

John Hewitt (1907-)

Denis Devlin (1908-1959)

Robert Farren (1909-)

W. R. Rodgers (1909-)

Leslie Daiken (1912-)

Donagh MacDonagh (1912-)

Valentin Iremonger (1918-)

Maurice Craig (1919-)

Robert Greacen (1920-)

Roy MacFadden (1921-)

Sean O Criadain (1930-)

Desmond O'Grady (1935-)

BOOKS FOR FURTHER READING

Thomas MacDonagh
Literature in Ireland (1916)

Ernest Boyd
Ireland's Literary Renaissance—second edition (1922)

Daniel Corkery
The Hidden Ireland (1925)

Aodh de Blacam
A First Book of Irish Literature (1934)

A. Rivoallan
Littérature Irlandaise Contemporaine (1939)

Robert Farren
The Course of Irish Verse (1948)

ANTHOLOGIES

Lennox Robinson (Ed.)
A Golden Treasury of Irish Verse (1925)

Seumas O'Sullivan (Ed.)
Editor's Choice. A Little Anthology of Poems selected from ' The Dublin Magazine ' (1944)

Geoffrey Taylor (Ed.)
*Irish Poems of To-day. Chosen from ' The Bell' * (1944)

Donagh MacDonagh (Ed.)
Poems from Ireland (1944)

Devin A. Garrity (Ed.)
New Irish Poets (1948)

Padriac Colum (Ed.)
Anthology of Irish Verse (1948)

Robert Greacen and Valentin Iremonger (Ed.)
Contemporary Irish Poetry (1949)

Donagh MacDonagh and Lennox Robinson (Ed.)
The Oxford Book of Irish Verse. XVIIth century to
XXth Century (1958)

saol agus cultúr
in éirinn

www.ingramcontent.com/pod-product-compliance
Lightning Source LLC
Chambersburg PA
CBHW052129150426
42813CB00077B/2640